Riding a Wave

Written by Susan Brocker

U.S.A.

My name is Mano. I live on the island of Oahu, in Hawaii. On weekends, I'm learning to surf. My class instructor is a professional surfer who has won many prizes. How do you think he teaches us to be safe in the ocean?

Contents

Look for the **Activity Zone!**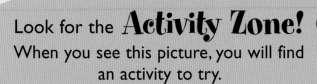
When you see this picture, you will find
an activity to try.

Catching a Wave

Hawaii is a chain of islands in the middle of the North Pacific Ocean. Its beautiful, sandy beaches offer some of the best surfing in the world.

Surfing is an exciting and challenging sport. Surfers need good balance, quick reflexes, and perfect timing. Most importantly, surfers need to understand the ever-changing sea. They need to know about different kinds of waves and how the waves act when they hit the beach. Knowledge of the ocean and its movements is vital to safe surfing.

The winters in Hawaii are not much cooler than the summers. It is hot enough to surf and swim there all year around.

reflex the body's first response to something we see, hear, smell, touch, or taste

The Hawaiian people have been surfing for at least 500 years. In the early 1900s, Hawaiian swimming champion Duke Kahanamoku introduced surfing to the world. Today, his memory is honored with this statue on Oahu island.

Hawaiian Shores

Different beaches on the Hawaiian islands have different kinds of surf. The northern shores face the wind, so the waves there can reach great heights. The southern shores are more sheltered, and the waves are gentler.

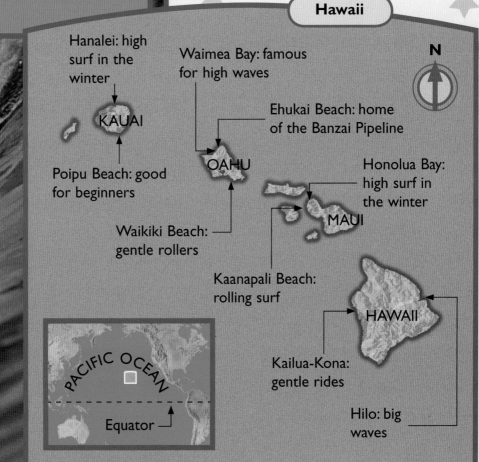

Hawaii

Hanalei: high surf in the winter

Waimea Bay: famous for high waves

Ehukai Beach: home of the Banzai Pipeline

KAUAI

Poipu Beach: good for beginners

OAHU

Honolua Bay: high surf in the winter

MAUI

Waikiki Beach: gentle rollers

Kaanapali Beach: rolling surf

HAWAII

Kailua-Kona: gentle rides

Hilo: big waves

N

PACIFIC OCEAN

Equator

Oceans in Motion

Oceans are never still. Their waters are constantly moving in giant streams called *currents*. The wind blowing across the ocean creates surface currents. Cold currents from the poles or warm currents from the equator move along shorelines, affecting the climates of the lands they pass.

Deep-water currents are caused by differences in water temperature and salt content. Cold, salty water sinks, while warm, less-salty water rises. This sets up a conveyor belt of deep, underwater currents from the poles to the equator.

RUSSIA

The wind blowing across the surface of the oceans creates currents of moving water that are about 330 feet deep.

CHINA

North Pacific Gyre

Hawaii

AUSTRALIA

Surface currents

South Indian Gyre

Surface currents move around the oceans in circular patterns called *gyres*. The wind is the major force driving these currents, but they are also affected by Earth's spin and the shape of the oceans. Currents in the Northern Hemisphere tend to circle clockwise, while those in the Southern Hemisphere circle counterclockwise.

hemisphere   one half of a globe, such as Earth

NORTH
AMERICA

Equator

SOUTH
AMERICA

South Pacific Gyre

Drifting Ducks

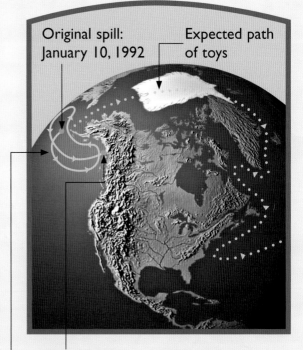

Original spill: January 10, 1992

Expected path of toys

Sitka, Alaska: First 400 toys found

Path of toys

In 1992, about 29,000 rubber ducks and other bathtub toys spilled overboard when a storm hit a cargo ship in the North Pacific Ocean. Since then, scientist Curt Ebbesmeyer has tracked the toys to learn more about ocean currents. To predict the course of the drifting ducks, he uses a computer model of ocean-current circulation called the *Ocean Surface Current Simulator*, or OSCURS.

Turning the Tide

Twice a day, the sea flows toward the shore and then ebbs back out again. This rise and fall of the ocean is called the *tide*. It is caused by the pull of gravity from the Moon. The Moon's gravity tugs at the ocean on the part of Earth that is nearer to it, causing the water to rise. As Earth spins, different parts of the ocean rise and fall.

The pull of gravity from the Sun also influences the tides. However, because the Sun is much farther from Earth, its pull is much weaker.

At low tide, many visitors to Marazion, England, walk to the nearby island of St. Michael's Mount. At high tide, they need a boat to reach the island.

gravity   the force that pulls all objects toward large objects, such as planets and moons

Highs and Lows

Honolulu Tides for April

Date	Low 1	High 1	Low 2	High 2
1	7.32 A.M.	12.03 A.M.	5.30 P.M.	12.54 P.M.
2	8.04 A.M.	12.47 A.M.	6.48 P.M.	1.35 P.M.
3	8.24 A.M.	1.36 A.M.	7.46 P.M.	2.16 P.M.
4	8.48 A.M.	2.13 A.M.	8.43 P.M.	3.00 P.M.

Tide charts tell us when the tide will be coming in and going out. Each day, the high and low tides are a little bit later than they were the day before.

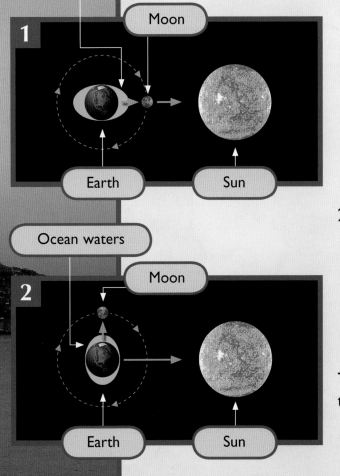

1. The highest high tides of all are called *spring tides*. They happen when Earth, the Moon, and the Sun are in line. At these times, the Moon's pull and the Sun's pull are combined.

2. The high tides that reach the least distance up the shore are called *neap tides*. They happen when the Sun and the Moon are at right angles and therefore pull in different directions.

There are two spring tides and two neap tides every month.

Making Waves

Most waves are formed by the wind blowing across the surface of the sea. The size of a wave depends on how far, how fast, and how long the wind blows. The stronger the wind, the higher the waves. Waves can travel thousands of miles across the ocean long after the wind has died away.

Unlike currents and tides, waves do not move water along. When a wave travels across the surface of the ocean, the water itself does not move forward. Instead, the water at each point moves up and down.

The big waves that pound Hawaiian shores start to build off the Aleutian Islands thousands of miles to the north. They reach Hawaii after about two days.

Scientists divide waves into parts to measure them.

The highest point of a wave is called the **crest**.

The lowest point is called the **trough**.

The vertical distance between the crest and the trough is the **wave height**.

The distance from one crest to the next is the **wavelength**.

Activity Zone!

1. Fill a tank with water and place a cork in the center.

2. Use masking tape to mark the position of the cork on the side of the tank.

3. At one end of the tank, lower and raise a small wooden block in and out of the water to make waves.

4. Notice how the cork bobs up and down but does not move forward. This is because waves move through water; they do not take the water with them.

Breaking Waves

When a wave nears land, water at the bottom of the wave drags on the seabed until the crest of the wave topples over and breaks onto the shore, creating surf.

Spilling breakers are a favorite with surfers. They form on gently sloping shores and roll a long way before breaking. Plunging breakers happen on beaches where the slope is steep. As the crest of the wave curls over, it creates a tunnel. Experienced surfers crouch under the curling crest and surf along the tube of water. Surging breakers often don't break at all. They form in deep water, often around rocks.

breaker a wave that is crashing onto the shore

Types of Breakers

As winter storms sweep across the Pacific, giant waves, nicknamed "jaws," crash onto Hawaii's northern shores. These waves can reach higher than 40 feet—far too high to paddle into. Surfers are towed out on jet skis. Only expert surfers can ride these waves.

Spilling breakers

Plunging breakers

Surging breakers

The Banzai Pipeline in Oahu, Hawaii, has spectacular, plunging breakers. When waves hit the steep reef that lies offshore, the swells slow down, and water piles up behind to form massive peaks, which then crash over.

13

Wild Water

Ocean waters can suddenly become wild and dangerous for several different reasons. Strong winds at sea can whip calm ocean waters into mountainous waves in minutes. The waves created by violent winds during particularly bad tropical storms can reach more than 45 feet high. When these waves hit land before the storm itself, they are called *storm surges*.

Colliding currents can also whip up ocean water. When the tide turns, currents sometimes crash into one another, creating a whirlpool.

When rising warm air meets falling cold air, it can form a spinning funnel that sucks up water from the sea into a waterspout.

Waterspouts are rare. They are tornadoes that form over oceans, pulling the water up into the spiraling air.

whirlpool   water that spirals rapidly into the center of a circle

The Beaufort Scale

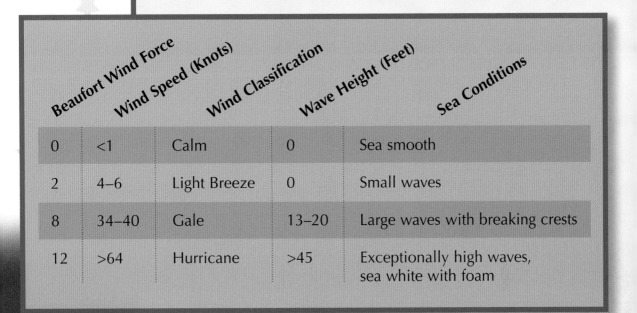

Beaufort Wind Force	Wind Speed (Knots)	Wind Classification	Wave Height (Feet)	Sea Conditions
0	<1	Calm	0	Sea smooth
2	4–6	Light Breeze	0	Small waves
8	34–40	Gale	13–20	Large waves with breaking crests
12	>64	Hurricane	>45	Exceptionally high waves, sea white with foam

The Beaufort Scale measures the force of wind at sea. At 0, the sea is calm; at 6, there is a strong breeze and large waves; at 12, there is a hurricane at full force, and the waves may be more than 45 feet high.

On September 11, 1992, Hurricane Iniki struck the island of Kauai in Hawaii. Huge waves and winds of up to 175 miles per hour battered the island. The hurricane caused more than two billion dollars worth of damage.

Tsunami Terror

Tsunamis are sometimes called *tidal waves*; however they have nothing to do with tides. They are enormous waves triggered by volcanic eruptions, earthquakes, or landslides that happen near or under the sea.

In the deep ocean, tsunamis are hardly noticed, because the water level rises without disturbing the surface. They travel vast distances at speeds of more than 500 miles an hour. When they approach shore, the shallow water acts as a brake, and they slow down and pile up into a gigantic wall of water. Finally, the wall of water surges across the land, destroying everything in its path.

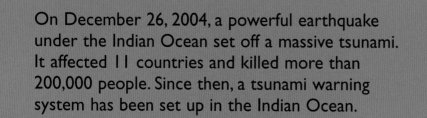

On December 26, 2004, a powerful earthquake under the Indian Ocean set off a massive tsunami. It affected 11 countries and killed more than 200,000 people. Since then, a tsunami warning system has been set up in the Indian Ocean.

Tilly Smith, a ten-year-old British schoolgirl, saved about 100 tourists from the tsunami that hit Thailand in 2004. She noticed that the tide was going out much faster and farther than normal—a sign of an approaching tsunami—and warned staff at the hotel where she was staying.

Pacific Warning System

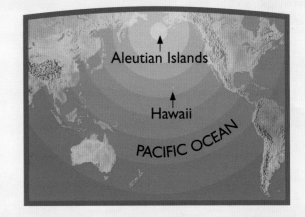

Aleutian Islands

Hawaii

PACIFIC OCEAN

On April 1, 1946, an earthquake shook the Aleutian Islands off the coast of Alaska. A tsunami then sped across the Pacific Ocean and struck Hawaii, killing more than 150 people. After this, a tsunami warning system was created in the Pacific Ocean. Research stations measure the height of tides and detect sudden changes in the water level. Special cables on the ocean floor sense when a tsunami wave passes over them.

Over the centuries, many tsunamis have struck harbors in Japan. *Tsunami* is a Japanese word that means "harbor wave."

Beach Hazards

To surfers and swimmers, the sea is a watery playground. However, the ocean is forever moving and changing, and it can be a dangerous place. Anyone entering the water or going on a boat trip should always check the sea conditions first and, if in doubt, stay out.

Strong rip currents often form when there are high waves and rapid tide changes. They can drag even strong swimmers out to sea. Nonetheless, swimmers and surfers can learn ways to keep safe in the water and still have a good time.

Even strong swimmers need to wear life jackets on boat trips. A life jacket keeps a person afloat even if he or she is too tired to keep swimming or has been knocked out.

rip current powerful channels of water flowing away from shore

Swimmers and beginner surfers visiting Hawaii often stay near Waikiki beach on Oahu. This beach faces south and is safe for swimming and surfing all year around.

Rip Currents

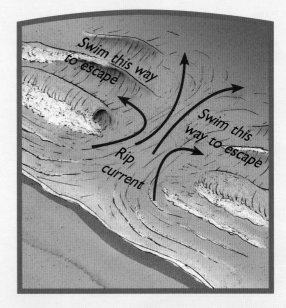

Rip currents are the major cause of drownings on surf beaches.

How to identify a rip current:
- a calm patch in the surf with waves breaking on each side
- a channel of churning, choppy water
- an area of differently colored water
- a line of foam, seaweed, or debris moving seaward

How to get out of a rip current:
- Stay calm and don't try to swim against the current.
- Swim to the side, until you reach the edge of the rip.
- Once in slower water, swim to shore.

Sea Sense

Even if you are not lucky enough to visit Hawaii, it is still a good idea to learn water safety. Many of the same rules apply whether you are in the sea, a lake, or a swimming pool.

The most important rule is to never swim alone. If no one sees a swimmer in need of help, then there is no hope of rescue for the swimmer. The safest places to swim are those patrolled by lifeguards. Remember, the sea is constantly changing, and even strong swimmers can get into trouble. Do not rely on a board or other floating device for safety.

Riding a short bodyboard can be a fun and easy introduction to surfing. A safety strap is linked to the wrist or ankle to prevent the board from becoming lost if the rider falls off.

These children attend water-safety classes once a week. Swimming lessons and water-safety classes are fun ways to learn how to keep safe in the water.

Be Water Wise

Expert surfers and swimmers know how to keep safe in the water. They follow these safety rules.

- Before you go in, ask a lifeguard if the water is safe for swimming.

- Look for and follow all safety signs.

- Never swim alone, and always make sure a responsible adult is watching you.

- Do not go swimming immediately after eating a big meal. Wait an hour for your food to settle.

- Wear sunscreen to prevent sunburn.

- Never swim in clothes made to be worn on dry land, because they become very heavy when they are wet.

Lifeguards to the Rescue

Lifeguards are strong swimmers specially trained in water rescue and first aid. They continually check the sea conditions and figure out the safest places for swimming. If a lifeguard is nearby, always choose to swim where he or she can see you.

If you get into difficulty in the sea, a lake, or a swimming pool, try to stay calm. Raise one arm into the air until a lifeguard reaches you. If you see someone else in trouble, throw in an object such as a life buoy to help the person stay afloat; then call for help.

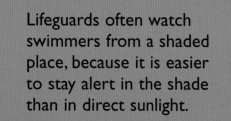

Lifeguards often watch swimmers from a shaded place, because it is easier to stay alert in the shade than in direct sunlight.

If a swimmer raises an arm out of the water, it means he or she is in trouble and needs help.

In addition to having a calm, responsible nature and being a strong swimmer, a lifeguard needs to know how to treat people who are injured or who start to drown. All lifeguards learn first aid, which teaches them how to take care of people until medical help arrives. You do not have to be a lifeguard to learn first aid, however. Courses are offered in most cities and towns and in many schools.

Some Hawaiian lifeguards patrol from a special raised room that allows them to see farther than they could on the ground.

23

Find Out More!

1   Where do you or people who
    live near you go swimming?
    What safety rules make
    swimming there safer?

2   Find out about the ocean currents
    that pass the shores of your country.
    Do they bring warm or cold water?

To find out more
about the ideas in
Riding a Wave, visit
www.researchit.org
on the web.

Index